FOURTEEN KEYS TO SUCCESSFUL FATHERING

FOURTEEN KEYS TO SUCCESSFUL FATHERING

KEN R. CANFIELD

MOODY PRESS

CHICAGO

ISBN: 0-8024-3711-7

1 3 5 7 9 10 8 6 4 2

Printed in the United States of America

If good fathering only called for common sense, there would be many more happy children. Successful fathering requires skill and commitment. This booklet offers fourteen insights or keys for becoming an effective father.

The insights in this booklet are derived from the research of the National Center for Fathering and from the author's own experience as the father of five busy children. Each of the fourteen keys appeard first as radio scripts for the daily broadcast "Today's Father," many of which were adapted from the book *The Seven Secrets of Effective Fathers*.

The booklet begins with challenging, encouraging calls to mastering fatherhood. Pastors, youth workers, and Mom are an incomplete team without Dad to help rear a child. God calls us to become master craftsmen of fathering. Practical action steps show every dad how to hone his skills.

Next come keys to improving a father's relationship with each of his children. Listening, maximizing bedtime, ideas for getting to know your children better than ever before. The final readings draw from sources as diverse as C. S. Lewis and farming in Kansas.

Each reading is motivational and practical for every father. With these fourteen keys, fathers will awaken to their high calling and find the first steps toward fulfilling that call.

Qualities of
Highly Committed Fathers

Imagine that somewhere, maybe in Cedar Rapids, Iowa, there lives the perfect father. He does everything right, and his kids are responsible and well adjusted. How does he do it? Or, perhaps more important, how does he keep going?

I'm convinced that that perfect father doesn't exist, but there are men out there who are taking steps to keep themselves highly motivated as fathers. I'm going to let you in on some of their secrets.

When I say the word *father*, what comes to your mind? Did you hear it as a noun or a verb—as a thing or an action? Highly committed fathers have a *task orientation* toward their role. For them, the word *father* is a noun and a verb. Let me explain the two concepts.

Those who view *father* as a noun see themselves as men filling a position, faithfully putting in their hours, fulfilling an obligation. But those who actively father their children view fathering as a life calling, something they are uniquely skilled to do.

Do you have goals at your office or work site? Then make goals at home and watch how it increases your motivation. Did you receive any training for your profession? Then learn effective parenting skills, and see how your confidence grows. Do you have a network of co-workers and colleagues who support your efforts in your career? Then create a network that includes your wife and Christian men who will support you in your fathering commitment.

Now maybe you're saying, "Sure, this fathering thing used to be fun, but now my kids are teenagers." These can be complex times. Maybe your daughter is embarrassed to be near you in public. Maybe your son looks at you and has absolutely nothing to say.

Brother, I'm praying for you. But I'm also here to tell you that now is the time when your kids most need you. Now is the time when your motivation as a father should be rising to its highest level.

Committed fathers find ways to overcome adversity and discouragement. They respond, change, adapt, and meet challenges. *They father.*

Fathers as Craftsmen

As I was growing up, I had the opportunity to work for some licensed craftsmen, mostly electricians and bricklayers. From watching Jerry, my bricklaying boss, I learned how to proportion the right amounts of mud, bricks, and wedges needed to complete a project. He'd get everything within easy reach so he could get in a rhythm, and he'd have hundreds of bricks perfectly in place in what seemed like no time.

Or take Curt, the electrician I worked for. He would carefully roll his wire out on the floor and unravel the kinks with his fingers before pulling it all smoothly through the conduit. Sometimes he even pumped soap into the pipe to make the pull easier.

Steps these craftsmen take make good sense after you've seen them done. You say, "Of course, that's the best way to do it." But though they make sense, they aren't necessarily common sense. In other words, if you were working alone, you probably wouldn't have set out to do it that way unless you had seen someone else do it or had been through the whole trial-and-error process yourself.

These craftsmen represent countless generations of experimentation, of a search for efficiency and *mastery*. They know "tricks of the trade" handed down from craftsman to apprentice, craftsman to apprentice. When you assist a craftsman you learn his secrets of the trade.

As fathers, you and I want to be craftsmen. We're apprentices who can *become* craftsmen. But we have to admit that any half-interested male graduate of puberty can father a child. A man I know says, "Anyone can make a kid, but it takes a man to be a father."

We need craftsmen. Anyone can hammer a nail into a board, but only a craftsman can build a cabinet, a house, or a home. In a newborn child, we have raw material that needs to be shaped and molded. Be a craftsman! Be skilled in your fathering! Produce in your family quality, usefulness, and beauty.

Our society has shown us that trial and error doesn't work in the craft of fathering. By the time we discover how to do things the best way, our children may be grown. So *now* is the time to commit. In order to become skilled craftsmen, we must all begin as apprentices. We need to turn to other wise and experienced fathers and ask them, "Show me how to do this and do it well. What are your secrets?" We need to learn how to be master craftsmen of fathering.

Fathers' Commitment Level

I'm sure many fathers have a deep desire to win with their kids, but, if you're like me, you have a difficult time staying motivated. You may learn insights and practical tips to help you become a better father, but they're only head knowledge if you never get around to carrying them out. You need ways to raise your motivation level and then sustain that high commitment to your kids. I have a few suggestions on how to do that.

First, take an aggressive approach. *Pursue high commitment.* I know that sounds rather foggy, but there are specific things you can do. For one thing, you can think about your commitment to your kids every day and verbalize it regularly. Say to each child, "I'm committed to you."

One father I know wrote down a list of his priorities—the things he felt called by God to do at that time in his life. He showed it to his son as a demonstration of how important he and the rest of the family were in his life. Such a pledge should not be used as a defense mechanism in case someone doubts your commitment, but instead as a sincere statement of your devotion.

Pursuing your commitment means planning on future commitment as your children grow. A father with a daughter just entering high school might say to himself, "Suzie's going to need a lot of my strength next year." In fact, he may even resolve to get up an hour earlier every morning to have a leisurely breakfast with Suzie and help her prepare for her day.

My second suggestion is, *monitor your commitment level closely.* Ask yourself, "Are my fathering responsibilities getting crowded out by other activities? Am I involving myself only in the discipline aspects and neglecting the fun, frivolous times with my kids?" A committed father can read his commitment level like a stockbroker reads the *Wall Street Journal.*

Third, when you do sense that your motivation tank is running on empty, refill it. Like every father, *you need a support group of other men* who will help keep you strong and hold you accountable. Besides the needed encouragement and wisdom you'll receive, the very fact that you are meeting regularly and faithfully with other dads will serve as another witness to your kids that you're committed to becoming the best father you can be.

Fathers and Spiritual Equipping

In 1988, Cynthia Clark did a study among families in which the parents were committed to passing on their religious beliefs to their children. She isolated firstborn, early adolescent sons to determine how each parent influenced these boys' religious beliefs. She found that mothers had more influence on their sons' *practical application* of religion, the day-to-day moments where faith comes alive. What do you suppose the fathers influenced? *Church attendance.*

What implications can we draw from this study? I would suggest that fathers tend to focus on their comfort zone—outer religious activity. The areas they tend to neglect, possibly because they feel inadequate, are the practical aspects of a deep, everyday commitment.

Why do so many of us feel inadequate when it comes to spiritual matters? Well, when you think about it, we're surrounded by people who seem better equipped to foster our children's growth—and it can be intimidating. There's the pastor, who's had years of training in the Bible. He seems to have the right answer for every situation. There's the youth minister, who strums a guitar and belts rap

13

tunes and finds a way to get through to our teens at a time when our relationship with them seems to be the most strained. Spiritual things even seem to come much more easily for our wives. They seem to have a more natural intimacy with Christ, and they can communicate it to our kids.

It's easy for us to be intimidated in spiritual matters, but we need to overcome our fears and embrace our God-given fatherly role as spiritual leader in the home. Do you have a wise pastor, a committed youth minister, and a faithful wife? Praise God for them, because they make your role that much easier. But you are still a vital part of this team.

A godly father and mother form a parenting team in which they complement each other to the benefit of the children. What you bring to the role of spiritual equipping will be different from what the mother brings —and your children need *both* of you.

Maybe you feel as though you're not a good enough Christian to be an effective spiritual equipper. I've always heard that the best way to learn something is to teach it to someone else. Since you haven't reached perfection, try the next best thing—*honesty*. Your honesty and transparency regarding the struggles in your spiritual life can teach your children much that a supposedly "perfect" father could not.

14

Drawing Confidence
from the Role of Father

Many of us fathers look at ourselves and say, "I'm really inadequate for this task." Maybe your father didn't show you any affection or never told you he was proud of you, and now you feel crippled in your own fathering. Maybe you were never around children until you had them yourself, and you're never quite sure you know what you're doing. These are valid excuses, but you also need to recognize the tremendous amount of power simply in the position of father.

We see positional power all the time with the president of the United States. On the campaign trail, congressmen of the opposing party will make it amazingly clear what an incompetent oaf they think their opponent in the White House is. And yet, they refer to him as "The President," and face-to-face they call him, "Mr. President." When he enters the House chambers to deliver the State of the Union address, they all rise to their feet and applaud.

Are they hypocrites? Perhaps. But they're also giving honor to the office of the presidency. They are indicating that they believe in that office as it has been outlined in the Constitution, as it was envisioned by the Founding Fathers.

When Dwight Eisenhower reviewed his troops before the Normandy Invasion, he could have worried that one of his privates would suddenly step out of rank and say, "Hey, wait a minute. You're just a farm boy from Abilene, Kansas. There's no way I'm going to hit that beach." But Eisenhower knew that the five stars on his helmet represented legitimate authority. His position gave him confidence to make the crucial orders to win the war.

There is similar power inherent in simply being a dad. Many effective fathers confess a sense of personal inadequacy. Yet however inadequate they feel, they have a great deal of confidence in the power of fatherhood.

Being a father is a marvelous thing—to give life and sustain life, and to sacrifice your own life for the sake of those who are helpless. We even use the title "father" to convey some of our greatest honors, whether it be to George Washington, the father of our country, or to God, our heavenly Father. The Father of all fathers has established faithful fathering as one of His essential tasks. We should all trust His design and follow His example.

16

Practical Tips
for Knowing Your Child

Truly effective fathers share one important quality. They make an effort to really get to know their children, and there are two major benefits to this. First of all, the process of getting to know our children intimately builds our relationships. We also want to gain the knowledge necessary to cultivate our children's unique gifts and talents, while protecting them from the dangers that our watchful eyes detect. Let me suggest five practical ways that each of us can gain this important knowledge about our children.

Number one is obvious, but some may be missing it. *Ask your child questions*. Take one of them out for a soda and ask about her friends at school—what she likes about her friends and what they like to do together. I must caution you not to turn this into an interrogation. Your child can tell whether you're genuinely interested or if you're simply collecting data to use against her later.

Number two: *Spend time on your child's turf*. Go to gymnastics classes and soccer practices. One day I went to watch my daughter Sarah's diving class. My other kids had been telling me how she was doing flips off the high dive, and, quite frankly, I found it a little hard to believe. But as I watched the class that day, I saw that they were right, and I also gained valuable insight into who my daughter is and how she thinks.

My third suggestion is, *provide your child with plenty of opportunities to discover personal interests and talents*. Now, I know how kids are: they change their minds and go from skating to gymnastics to the violin, and as fathers we have to soak up the cost. We are allowing our children to explore their interests and find out what they are really good at. We need to remember not to place high expectations on them. The goal is not performance, it's discovery.

Number four: *Give your child feedback, especially praise*. I'm not saying you should critique everything your child does. Instead, praise your child for his effort, and tell him your positive observations. In doing so, you give him the chance to explain his point of view, and you learn even more.

Finally, let me urge you to *listen to your child's friends, his teachers, his coaches and, especially, his mother*. All of these people see a side of your child that you do not, and they can often provide you with insights you would have never gained. As you get really brave, I recommend asking your wife for feedback about your relationship with each child.

When we know our children intimately, we are much more prepared to do what is best for them.

Listening Perseverance

Rose is an elderly woman I've been caring for over the years. She is ninety-three years old. Each week when I stop by the rest home where she lives, she insists on telling me her repertoire of stories. These stories are not new. Most of them come from events forty or fifty years ago, and I've heard them probably a hundred times.

One day, as I was listening to her stories, I noticed something in the way she was watching me. I could tell that she was no longer concentrating on the story at all, but she was watching me, to see if I was still listening. I imagine that deep down inside, she was thinking something like this: *Ken, I know I'm old and that I've told these stories so many times that I've begun to mix their details. But if you listen closely, they will tell you who I am. They are all I have. Will you care for me enough to listen, even when I lapse into gibberish?*

I tell you about Rose because elderly people, in some ways, are like children. Much of what our children tell us may seem unimportant. When they begin to speak of how they view the world, their thoughts may be hopelessly inaccurate or shallow or silly. We need to realize that the value is not so much in what is said, but in the saying of it and being heard. When we actively listen to our children, we say "I love you" without even speaking a word.

Micah is the storyteller in our family. When we are driving home from a movie, he sits in the back of the van so that all can hear him, and he recounts the entire story, even though we were all with him in the theater just minutes before. The next day I'll get another recap: "Dad, wasn't it great when that car wrecked into that truck and all those chickens went flying around?" There are things that I can learn about Micah even from his monotonous reruns, and for him it doesn't matter so much what he is telling me or that I respond wisely. For now, Micah is pleased by my listening.

This chitchat may seem pretty tedious to you now, but please remember that you're proving yourself as a concerned, active listener. As much as some of us would like to forget, the teenage years are coming. If your child learns that you're open and attentive to the small things, he'll be much more willing to come to you when he's facing his biggest struggles or making his toughest decisions.

Active Listening

Our homes can be very noisy places. The television blares. The washing machine rattles and bumps. The microwave beeps. The kids come rumbling through the living room and out the front door. But there's other noise.

There's the checkbook voicing its demands: "You gotta pay the bills." The job stands outside and taps incessantly on the window, calling, "Hey, pay attention to me." The clock in the hallway ticks loudly enough to remind us of all we have to do and how little time we have in which to do it.

A home can be a noisy place. And that's unfortunate. Because beneath all the noise, there are some softly spoken whispers that need to be heard. These tiny voices peep quietly, "Listen to me, please. I have something important to say." But they often go unnoticed amid the racket. These are the tiny voices of our children.

At this point you're probably saying, "Wait a minute, my kids are anything but quiet."

Your children may not seem quiet, but the tiny voices I'm talking about do not originate in their lungs. These whispers come from even deeper—

from the heart. In a hundred different ways your children try to communicate who they are, what they feel, what they fear, who they love, how they think, why they cry, what they hope for, and where they hurt. Your children want you to know who they are so that you can accept them fully. And they want to tell you where it hurts so that you can fix it.

Too often the important tiny voices of our children get lost beneath adult noise. We figure that the only way to gain control of the hubbub is to shout loudly enough to be heard above it. So we add to the racket: "Do this!" we scream. "Don't do that!" we yell. How many times have you started a conversation with: "Here's what you need to do . . ." Or, "Let me give you some advice . . ." Or better yet, "When I was your age . . ."

But there's a lot we can do to turn down the decibels. For example, we can turn off the TV and put away distractions. Most important, we can train ourselves to be slow to speak and quick to listen.

File away the lectures for another day, and let our children speak instead. Some noise may seem beyond our control, but even then we can learn to tune out the noise and focus our attention for those times when we especially need to listen to our children.

23

Bedtime

Here is what a first-grader wrote about her dad in one of our essay contests:

> At night before bed we talk about our day and if I am sad or scared he always makes me feel good before going to sleep because he reminds me of the good things that happened.

It's actually surprising that when we ask kids to write about their fathers, many of them choose to say something about bedtime.

To try to understand what our children are going through, all we have to do is remember when we were their age. There were monsters trampling through our dreams too, and strange shapes on the walls of our bedrooms.

As fathers, we can have a profound effect on our kids' state of mind as they drift into sleep every night. Our children look to us for strength and security, and too many us get so caught up in hustling n through baths and getting into bed on time that we miss e opportunities to build rela- with our children.

Bedtime is when your kids will be their most receptive to you, even if their only motivation is staying up for another fifteen minutes. We can use that time to put a period at the end of the day, to help our children gain a healthy perspective on the positives and negatives that they have experienced. We can help them sort out their feelings and set a positive tone for whatever tomorrow will bring.

Most of all, bedtime is a perfect chance to speak the words of blessing that all children need so desperately to hear. What better way to punctuate the end of children's days than to affirm them for who they are as our beloved children, in whom we are well pleased.

Listen to what a firstgrader named Nicholas wrote about his dad:

> He gets home late but I still feel his big strong hands put the sign of the cross on my forehead saying "God bless." Then he leans to my ear and whispers, "Sleep with angels, son. Daddy loves you."

Family Devotions

These two words strike fear into the hearts of Christian fathers all over the nation. I've heard many men say they want to have a regular time when they gather the family together to read the Bible, sing, and pray as a family. But invariably they ask me, "How do I do it?" And when they do start daily devotions, their commitment doesn't last more than a few weeks.

Let me offer you a few words of encouragement. Family devotions do not have to be slick productions that take hours of preparation. And don't feel like you need to come up with theological insight on the level of your pastor's Sunday sermon. There is an ever-increasing supply of resources, including daily devotional books, that make the entire process much less complex than many fathers imagine. Your children will be influenced more by your commitment to make worship a regular part of your family life than they will by your profound exegesis of Scripture.

This regularity is possibly the most important feature of your family devotions. You must convince your children that you'll be having family devotions *every day*, not only when it's convenient or when there's nothing better to do. It's also good to schedule a regular time for the family to gather. For some, the best time is right before or after breakfast; for others, the kids are most receptive right before bed. But if you allow your devotions to jump around from day to day you'll be sending the message that your faith depends on your moods or your busy schedule. *Consistency is the key.*

I know what you're thinking. If you commit to devotions every single day, you'll never keep your kids' attention—or your own enthusiasm—for very long. This is where the second most important feature comes in. I'm talking about *flexibility.*

Your flexibility will make these times more enjoyable and beneficial for the entire family. Maybe you spend a month reading through a book of the Bible, then switch to a devotional book. Or you can read through a biography of a Christian leader who learned to apply important biblical truths to his life. Some days you may want to just talk about how God has blessed your family, and maybe you'll set special traditions for birthdays and holidays.

You don't have to have the charisma of a famous singer or preacher to win at family devotions. And I think you'll be surprised at how well your kids respond when you demonstrate consistency and flexibility.

C. S. Lewis on Fatherhood

I hold C. S. Lewis in very high esteem. He is the creator of such memorable characters as Aslan the lion and Screwtape the supervisory demon. His book *Mere Christianity* is considered a classic of Christian apologetics. Yet I've wondered where Lewis's wisdom comes from, for those who normally establish a person in the world—one's parents—were taken from him.

When C. S. Lewis was still a young boy, his mother died of cancer. His father suffered the grief harshly, and Lewis writes, "Under the pressure of anxiety [my father's] temper became incalculable; he spoke wildly and acted unjustly. Thus by a peculiar cruelty of fate, during those months the unfortunate man . . . was really losing his sons as well as his wife." Shortly thereafter, as was common in the British Empire, Lewis was shipped off to boarding school. The Irish Channel separated him and his father.

Lewis found his footing by seeking out other fathers—surrogate fathers—and perhaps none so powerful in his life as the Scottish author George MacDonald. Even though MacDonald had lived in the previous century, Lewis read MacDonald's books as an attentive son listening to his father. "I have never concealed the fact that I regarded him as my master," Lewis declares.

When it came time to summarize what he had learned from MacDonald, C. S. Lewis thought about his own childhood by comparison and made this comment: "An almost perfect relationship with his father was the earthly root of all [George MacDonald's] wisdom. From his own father, [MacDonald] said, he first learned that fatherhood must be at the core of the universe."

Fatherhood—the root of all earthly wisdom? Fatherhood—at the core of the universe? Those are bold statements. C. S. Lewis obviously longed for something he never received in his childhood, and that leads me to ask this question on behalf of your children: "Should fatherhood be at the core of *your* universe?" When you think about all the tasks to which you are devoting your life, do you ever get the sense that what you do as a father will have the greatest lasting impact and provide you with the deepest personal satisfaction?

And what of those children in our neighborhoods who are fatherless? Effective fathers reach out beyond the four walls of their homes to touch those who need to know the power of a father. One hundred fifty years ago in the Scottish Highlands, one man committed himself to being an effective father. He can count C. S. Lewis among his spiritual grandchildren.

Parental Discussion

One of your greatest assets as a father is your teammate—your wife. I'm not talking about her feeding the kids and changing their diapers and dressing them and then giving them to you to play with. That's hardly teamwork.

The kind of teamwork I'm thinking of isn't even like a well-disciplined eleven-man offense moving a football ninety yards to score. It isn't having a secret weapon come in for a fourth-and-long desperation play. That would be like having your wife come in and father your children for you when you start thinking you can't handle it. However good your wife might be as a mother, she cannot be a father to your children. Only *you* can be a father.

The kind of teamwork I'm picturing is more like halftime in the locker room. Coaches review the statistics, talk about what the players are and aren't doing well, and give encouragement for the next half. In fathering, we call it *parental discussion*, and more and more of us are reaping its benefits. We compare notes, ask for feedback on how we're doing, and gather the strength to love our kids through whatever struggles may arise tomorrow. I have identified three things that a wise father can gain from discussion with his wife.

First, she can provide you with *information* about your children. She is with your children in situations where you cannot be. So when the kids are finally settled quietly in bed, you can hear her stories about what happened and how your children reacted, and gain that much more knowledge about who your kids are.

Along with that, your wife can also provide you with *a different perspective* on your children. You see only one portion of your child's life— *your* perspective. Your wife has a completely different perspective, and it can be quite illuminating to compare notes. She'll be especially helpful when it comes to understanding your growing daughters.

The third way you can benefit from regular discussion with your wife is that you'll notice an *improvement in your own parenting skills*. Mothers are naturally sensitive to the needs of their children and how to meet those needs, and that sensitivity makes them the most knowledgeable experts on your kids. Ask her for advice, and listen. Or get her to sit down, look her in the eye, and ask, "Honey, how am I doing?"

As a wise father, you realize that you are not alone, and through parental discussion you and your wife can form a parenting team that can work effectively for the benefit of your children.

Responding to Crises

Several summers ago, my youngest son Micah rode his three-wheeler into the street in front of our house and was hit by a car. His left leg was broken in two places, and as I stood there in the hospital next to his bed, the thoughts raced through my head: Why was he riding alone next to the street? Why couldn't I protect him?

Well, Micah's OK, and I think he learned his lesson. But perhaps the greatest lessons of the incident were reserved for me, his father. I learned how dangerous this world can be for those I love. Crises will happen in my family, and I need to be prepared to respond to them.

As fathers, we cannot always prevent these things from happening, but our actions can do a lot to determine the outcome when a crisis does occur. I'd like to give you four things you can do to make you a better protector of your children:

First, *adopt a healthy attitude toward crises.* Realize that those things will happen and that it is your role as a father to take a leadership role in resolving a crisis. Also, remember that your family can gain strength from the crisis, strength that will far outweigh the harm suffered.

The second way you can prepare yourself is to *understand your own foundation as a man.* In our research at the National Center for Fathering, fathers who scored high in being able to deal with crises also scored significantly higher on their responses to "male identity" issues. We can take confidence in how God has created us. When crises occur, say to yourself, "It is for occasions just like this that I was made a man and a father."

Third, *maintain healthy communication with your kids.* The father who deals successfully with crises has healthy verbal interaction with his kids. He is able to talk things through, during and after a crisis. He can openly communicate with his children, and his children feel they have an open channel to their dad at any time, concerning any subject.

My final word of advice is to *maintain healthy discussion habits with your wife.* When a crisis occurs to parents who communicate openly with one another, they are able to get positive results both as a couple and with their children. For this couple, discussion will be a natural response in times of crisis, and a father will be able to utilize the strengths that both partners bring to the marital team.

Farmers and Fathers

Stretching in all directions from my home in Kansas lies some of the most fertile farmland in the nation. The farmers here produce grain—mainly wheat. In late June, the fields are like a sea of gold.

What brought about this bounty?

You could ask the farmers, and they might tell you about the ground: how to prepare it, how to rotate crops. They could tell you about the seed and about planting seasons and fertilizer and herbicide and irrigation.

"Yeah, but what caused this crop to grow so well?" you ask.

"I just told you," the old farmer says, "Good soil, high-quality seed, proper cultivation . . ."

"No, what caused this crop to grow at all?"

"It just happens," one farmer says.

"God causes it," says another one.

A third man volunteers, "It's really a mystery. We do what we can, but you never can tell when a drought's going to ruin us, or when we'll have more rain than we can handle. It's ultimately beyond our control."

As fathers, we have to admit that there's no guarantee our children will turn out the way we want them to. They are human beings who will make their own choices. They'll disappoint us in some ways, and they'll accomplish things that we never would have thought possible. Hopefully we've equipped them to handle the environment where wise choices come naturally. But the *choosing* still belongs to our children. We can influence and shape their lives, but we can never control them.

Suppose you approached one of these farmers and asked, "What would you expect to happen at harvest time if you chose good soil and planted the appropriate seed and if you fertilized to the right degree and irrigated as necessary? If you faithfully employed all you know about good farming, what would happen?"

The farmer says, "It's likely I'd have a good harvest, but there are still too many things beyond my control."

But then you could ask the farmer this: "What if you decide to do nothing at all? What if you don't plow and disk the soil? What if you don't plant any seed or apply any herbicide or irrigate the fields? What would you expect to happen."

"Oh, then I *know* what would happen," the farmer says. "I'd be shooting myself in the foot—guaranteeing my own failure."

So it is with fathering. We can apply what we've learned from books or from other men or from our own experiences, and it's likely we'll reap a crop of well-equipped children who live their lives wonderfully before God—realizing ourselves that there are no guarantees. We all need to apply what we know about effective fathering and humbly trust God for the rest.

The National Center for Fathering is a research and education group committed to "championing the role of fathering, and equipping men through research and education." For more information on seminars and fathering resources or for a free copy of the Center's newsletter, *Today's Father*, call 1-800-593-DADS.